TABLE OF CONTENTS

Secret Key #1 – Time is Your Greatest Enemy

To succeed on the secretary exam, you must use your time wisely. Most people do not finish at least one section. The time constraints are brutal. To succeed, you must ration your time properly.

On every section the test is separated into passages. The reason that time is so critical is that 1) every question counts the same toward your final score, and 2) the passages are not in order of difficulty. If you have to rush during the last passage, then you will miss out on answering easier questions correctly. It is natural to want to pause and figure out the hardest questions, but you must resist the temptation and move quickly.

Success Strategy #1

Wear a watch to the secretary exam. At the beginning of the test, check the time (or start a chronometer on your watch to count the minutes), and check the time after each passage to make sure you are "on schedule."

If you find that you are behind time during the test, work through the next passage more quickly. If you are still behind time after the next passage, skip the last question of the following passage in an attempt to catch up (unless you know it at a quick glance). Once you are caught up, maintain that pace until the end of the test.

The Math Section is the easiest to keep time on; move on if you take more than a minute on a question. If you have time left over, come back to the earliest skipped questions, spend another minute at most, and then move on to the next skipped question.

Last minute guessing will be covered in the next chapter.

The Reading section poses the greatest challenge for time. Unless you are an uncommonly fast reader, I strongly suggest you follow our advice in the Reading Section covered later in the guide- focus on the questions, and scan for answers as necessary.

Lastly, sometimes it is beneficial to slow down if you are constantly getting ahead of time. You are always more likely to catch a careless mistake by working more slowly than quickly, and among very high-scoring people (those who are likely to have lots of time left over), careless errors affect the score more than mastery of material.

Secret Key #2 – Guessing is Not Guesswork

You probably know that guessing is a good idea on the secretary exam – unlike most tests; there is no penalty for getting a wrong answer. Even if you have no idea about a question, you still have a 20-25% chance of getting it right.

Monkeys Take the Secretary Exam

What most people don't realize is that to insure that 20-25% chance, you have to guess randomly. If you put 20 monkeys in a room to take the secretary exam, assuming they answered once per question and behaved themselves, on average they would get 20-25% of the questions correct. Put 20 people in the room, and the average will be much lower among guessed questions. Why?

Secretary exams are intentionally written with deceptive answer choices that "look" right. An average person has no idea about a question, so picks the "best looking" answer, which is often wrong. The monkey has no idea what looks good and what doesn't, so will consistently be lucky about 20-25% of the time.

People will eliminate answer choices from the guessing pool based on a hunch or intuition. Simple but correct answers often get excluded, leaving a 0% chance of being correct. The monkey has no clue, and often gets lucky with the best choice.

This is why the process of elimination endorsed by most test courses is flawed and detrimental to your performance- people don't guess, they make an ignorant stab in the dark that is usually worse than random.

Success Strategy #2

Let me introduce one of the most valuable ideas of this course- the $5 challenge:

You only mark your "best guess" if you are willing to bet $5 on it.
You only eliminate choices from guessing if you are willing to bet $5 on it.

Why $5? Five dollars is an amount of money that is small yet not insignificant, and can really add up fast (20 questions could cost you $100). Likewise, each answer choice on one question of the secretary exam will have a small impact on your overall score, but it can really add up to a lot of points in the end.

The process of elimination IS valuable. However, if you accidentally eliminate the right answer or go on a hunch for an incorrect answer, your chances drop dramatically: to 0%. By guessing among all the answer choices, you are GUARANTEED to have a shot at the right answer.

That's why the $5 test is so valuable- if you give up the advantage and safety of a pure guess, it had better be worth the risk.

What we still haven't covered is how to be sure that whatever guess you make is truly random. Here's the easiest way:

Always pick the first answer choice among those remaining.

Such a technique means that you have decided, **before you see a single test question**, exactly how you are going to guess- and since the order of choices tells you nothing about which one is correct, this guessing technique is perfectly random.

Let's try an example-

A person encounters the following problem on the math section:
What is ½ divided by ¾ equal to?

A. 1

B. 2/3

C. 3/8

D. 3/2

E. 8/4

The person has a small idea about this question- he is pretty sure that he needs to either multiply across or either take the inverse and multiply across, but he wouldn't bet $5 on either method. He knows that in division you somehow multiply across so he is willing to bet $5 on both choices A and E not being correct. So he is down to B, C, and D. At this point, he guesses B, since B is the first choice remaining.

The person is correct by choosing B, since you do flip the second fraction and multiply straight across from there. He only eliminated those choices he was willing to bet money on, AND he did not let his stale memories (often things not known definitely will get mixed up in the exact opposite arrangement in one's head) influence his guess. He blindly chose the first remaining choice, and was rewarded with the fruits of a random guess.

This section is not meant to scare you away from making educated guesses or eliminating choices- you just need to define when a choice is worth eliminating. The $5 test, along with a pre-defined random guessing strategy, is the best way to make sure you reap all of the benefits of guessing.

Secret Key #3 –Practice Smarter, Not Harder

Many people delay the test preparation process because they dread the awful amounts of practice time they think necessary to succeed on the test. We have refined an effective method that will take you only a fraction of the time.

There are a number of "obstacles" in your way on the secretary exam. Among these are answering questions, finishing in time, and mastering test-taking strategies. All must be executed on the day of the test at peak performance, or your score will suffer. The secretary exam is a mental marathon that has a large impact on your future.

Just like a marathon runner, it is important to work your way up to the full challenge. So first you just worry about questions, and then time, and finally strategy:

Success Strategy #3

1. Find a good source for secretary exam practice tests.
2. If you are willing to make a larger time investment, consider using more than one study guide- often the different approaches of multiple authors will help you "get" difficult concepts.
3. Take a practice test with no time constraints, with all study helps "open book." Take your time with questions and focus on applying the strategies.
4. Take another test, this time with time constraints, with all guides "open book."
5. Take a final practice test with no open material and time limits.

If you have time to take more practice tests, just repeat step 5. By gradually exposing yourself to the full rigors of the test environment, you will condition your mind to the stress of test day and maximize your success.

Secret Key #4 - Prepare, Don't Procrastinate

Let me state an obvious fact: if you take the test three times, you will get three different scores. This is due to the way you feel on test day, the level of preparedness you have, and, despite the test writers' claims to the contrary, some tests WILL be easier for you than others.

Since your future depends so much on your score, you should maximize your chances of success. In order to maximize the likelihood of success, you've got to prepare in advance. This means taking practice tests and spending time learning the information and test taking strategies you will need to succeed.

Never take the test as a "practice" test, expecting that you can just take it again if you need to. Feel free to take sample tests on your own, but when you go to take the official test, be prepared, be focused, and do your best the first time!

Secret Key #5 - Test Yourself

Everyone knows that time is money. There is no need to spend too much of your time or too little of your time preparing for the test. You should only spend as much of your precious time preparing as is necessary for you to get the score you need.

Once you have taken a practice test under real conditions of time constraints, then you will know if you are ready for the test or not.

If you have scored extremely high the first time that you take the practice test, then there is not much point in spending countless hours studying. You are already there.

Benchmark your abilities by retaking practice tests and seeing how much you have improved. Once you score high enough to guarantee success, then you are ready.

If you have scored well below where you need, then knuckle down and begin studying in earnest. Check your improvement regularly through the use of practice tests under real conditions. Above all, don't worry, panic, or give up. The key is perseverance!

Then, when you go to take the test, remain confident and remember how well you did on the practice tests. If you can score high enough on a practice test, then you can do the same on the real thing.

Top 20 Test Taking Tips

1. Carefully follow all the test registration procedures
2. Know the test directions, duration, topics, question types, how many questions
3. Setup a flexible study schedule at least 3-4 weeks before test day
4. Study during the time of day you are most alert, relaxed, and stress free
5. Maximize your learning style; visual learner use visual study aids, auditory learner use auditory study aids
6. Focus on your weakest knowledge base
7. Find a study partner to review with and help clarify questions
8. Practice, practice, practice
9. Get a good night's sleep; don't try to cram the night before the test
10. Eat a well balanced meal
11. Know the exact physical location of the testing site; drive the route to the site prior to test day
12. Bring a set of ear plugs; the testing center could be noisy
13. Wear comfortable, loose fitting, layered clothing to the testing center; prepare for it to be either cold or hot during the test
14. Bring at least 2 current forms of ID to the testing center
15. Arrive to the test early; be prepared to wait and be patient
16. Eliminate the obviously wrong answer choices, then guess the first remaining choice
17. Pace yourself; don't rush, but keep working and move on if you get stuck
18. Maintain a positive attitude even if the test is going poorly
19. Keep your first answer unless you are positive it is wrong
20. Check your work, don't make a careless mistake

General Strategies

The most important thing you can do is to ignore your fears and jump into the test immediately- do not be overwhelmed by any strange-sounding terms. You have to jump into the test like jumping into a pool- all at once is the easiest way.

Make Predictions

As you read and understand the question, try to guess what the answer will be. Remember that several of the answer choices are wrong, and once you begin reading them, your mind will immediately become cluttered with answer choices designed to throw you off. Your mind is typically the most focused immediately after you have read the question and digested its contents. If you can, try to predict what the correct answer will be. You may be surprised at what you can predict.

Quickly scan the choices and see if your prediction is in the listed answer choices. If it is, then you can be quite confident that you have the right answer. It still won't hurt to check the other answer choices, but most of the time, you've got it!

Answer the Question

It may seem obvious to only pick answer choices that answer the question, but the test writers can create some excellent answer choices that are wrong. Don't pick an answer just because it sounds right, or you believe it to be true. It MUST answer the question. Once you've made your selection, always go back and check it against the question and make sure that you didn't misread the question, and the answer choice does answer the question posed.

Benchmark

After you read the first answer choice, decide if you think it sounds correct or not. If it doesn't, move on to the next answer choice. If it does, mentally mark that answer choice. This doesn't mean that you've definitely selected it as your answer choice, it just means that it's the best you've seen thus far. Go ahead and read the next choice. If the next choice is worse than the one you've already selected, keep going to the next answer choice. If the next choice is better than the choice you've already selected, mentally mark the new answer choice as your best guess.

The first answer choice that you select becomes your standard. Every other answer choice must be benchmarked against that standard. That choice is correct until proven otherwise by another answer choice beating it out. Once you've decided that no other answer choice seems as good, do one final check to ensure that your answer choice answers the question posed.

Valid Information

Don't discount any of the information provided in the question. Every piece of information may be necessary to determine the correct answer. None of the information in the question is there to throw you off (while the answer choices will certainly have information to throw you off). If two seemingly unrelated topics are discussed, don't ignore either. You can be confident there is a relationship, or it wouldn't be included in the question, and you are probably going to have to determine what is that relationship to find the answer.

Avoid "Fact Traps"

Don't get distracted by a choice that is factually true. Your search is for the answer that answers the question. Stay focused and don't fall for an answer that is true but incorrect. Always go back to the question and make sure you're choosing an answer that actually answers the question and is not just a true statement. An answer can be factually correct, but it MUST answer the question asked. Additionally, two answers can both be seemingly correct, so be sure to read all of the answer choices, and make sure that you get the one that BEST answers the question.

Milk the Question

Some of the questions may throw you completely off. They might deal with a subject you have not been exposed to, or one that you haven't reviewed in years. While your lack of knowledge about the subject will be a hindrance, the question itself can give you many clues that will help you find the correct answer. Read the question carefully and look for clues. Watch particularly for adjectives and nouns describing difficult terms or words that you don't recognize. Regardless of if you completely understand a word or not, replacing it with a synonym either provided or one you more familiar with may help you to understand what the questions are asking. Rather than wracking your mind about specific detailed information concerning a difficult term or word, try to use mental substitutes that are easier to understand.

The Trap of Familiarity

Don't just choose a word because you recognize it. On difficult questions, you may not recognize a number of words in the answer choices. The test writers don't put "make-believe" words on the test; so don't think that just because you only recognize all the words in one answer choice means that answer choice must be correct. If you only recognize words in one answer choice, then focus on that one. Is it correct? Try your best to determine if it is correct. If it is, that is great, but if it doesn't, eliminate it. Each word and answer choice you eliminate increases your chances of getting the question correct, even if you then have to guess among the unfamiliar choices.

Eliminate Answers

Eliminate choices as soon as you realize they are wrong. But be careful! Make sure you consider all of the possible answer choices. Just because one appears right, doesn't mean that the next one won't be even better! The test writers will usually put more than one good answer choice for every question, so read all of them. Don't worry if you are stuck between two that seem right. By getting down to just two remaining possible choices, your odds are now 50/50. Rather than wasting too much time, play the odds. You are guessing, but guessing wisely, because you've been able to knock out some of the answer choices that you know are wrong. If you are eliminating choices and realize that the last answer choice you are left with is also obviously wrong, don't panic. Start over and consider each choice again. There may easily be something that you missed the first time and will realize on the second pass.

Tough Questions

If you are stumped on a problem or it appears too hard or too difficult, don't waste time. Move on! Remember though, if you can quickly check for obviously incorrect answer choices, your chances of guessing correctly are greatly improved. Before you completely give up, at least try to knock out a couple of possible answers. Eliminate what you can and then guess at the remaining answer choices before moving on.

Brainstorm

If you get stuck on a difficult question, spend a few seconds quickly brainstorming. Run through the complete list of possible answer choices. Look at each choice and ask yourself, "Could this answer the question satisfactorily?" Go through each answer choice and consider it independently of the other. By systematically going through all possibilities, you may find something that you would otherwise overlook. Remember that when you get stuck, it's important to try to keep moving.

Read Carefully

Understand the problem. Read the question and answer choices carefully. Don't miss the question because you misread the terms. You have plenty of time to read each question thoroughly and make sure you understand what is being asked. Yet a happy medium must be attained, so don't waste too much time. You must read carefully, but efficiently.

Face Value

When in doubt, use common sense. Always accept the situation in the problem at face value. Don't read too much into it. These problems will not require you to make huge leaps of logic. The test writers aren't trying to throw you off with a cheap trick. If you have to go beyond creativity and make a leap of logic in order to have an answer choice answer the question, then you should look at the other answer choices. Don't overcomplicate the problem by creating theoretical relationships or explanations that will warp time or space. These are normal problems rooted in reality. It's just that the applicable relationship or explanation may not be readily apparent and you have to figure things out. Use your common sense to interpret anything that isn't clear.

Prefixes

If you're having trouble with a word in the question or answer choices, try dissecting it. Take advantage of every clue that the word might include. Prefixes and suffixes can be a huge help. Usually they allow you to determine a basic meaning. Pre- means before, post- means after, pro - is positive, de- is negative. From these prefixes and suffixes, you can get an idea of the general meaning of the word and try to put it into context. Beware though of any traps. Just because con is the opposite of pro, doesn't necessarily mean congress is the opposite of progress!

Hedge Phrases

Watch out for critical "hedge" phrases, such as likely, may, can, will often, sometimes, often, almost, mostly, usually, generally, rarely, sometimes. Question writers insert these hedge phrases to cover every possibility. Often an answer choice will be wrong simply because it leaves no room for exception. Avoid answer choices that have definitive words like "exactly," and "always".

Switchback Words

Stay alert for "switchbacks". These are the words and phrases frequently used to alert you to shifts in thought. The most common switchback word is "but". Others include although, however, nevertheless, on the other hand, even though, while, in spite of, despite, regardless of.

New Information

Correct answer choices will rarely have completely new information included. Answer choices typically are straightforward reflections of the material asked about and will directly relate to the question. If a new piece of information is included in an answer choice that doesn't even seem to relate to the topic being asked about, then that answer choice is likely incorrect. All of the information needed to answer the question is usually provided for you, and so you should not have to make guesses that are unsupported or choose answer choices that require unknown information that cannot be reasoned on its own.

Time Management

On technical questions, don't get lost on the technical terms. Don't spend too much time on any one question. If you don't know what a term means, then since you don't have a dictionary, odds are you aren't going to get much further. You should immediately recognize terms as whether or not you know them. If you don't, work with the other clues that you have, the other answer choices and terms provided, but don't waste too much time trying to figure out a difficult term.

Contextual Clues

Look for contextual clues. An answer can be right but not correct. The contextual clues will help you find the answer that is most right and is correct. Understand the context in which a phrase or statement is made. This will help you make important distinctions.

Don't Panic

Panicking will not answer any questions for you. Therefore, it isn't helpful. When you first see the question, if your mind goes blank, take a deep breath. Force yourself to mechanically go through the steps of solving the problem and using the strategies you've learned.

Pace Yourself

Don't get clock fever. It's easy to be overwhelmed when you're looking at a page full of questions, your mind is full of random thoughts and feeling confused, and the clock is ticking down faster than you would like. Calm down and maintain the pace that you have set for yourself. As long as you are on track by monitoring your pace, you are guaranteed to have enough time for yourself. When you get to the last few minutes of the test, it may seem like you won't have enough time left, but if you only have as many questions as you should have left at that point, then you're right on track!

Answer Selection

The best way to pick an answer choice is to eliminate all of those that are wrong, until only one is left and confirm that is the correct answer. Sometimes though, an answer choice may immediately look right. Be careful! Take a second to make sure that the other choices are not equally obvious. Don't make a hasty mistake. There are only two times that you should stop before checking other answers. First is when you are positive that the answer choice you have selected is correct. Second is when time is almost out and you have to make a quick guess!

Check Your Work

Since you will probably not know every term listed and the answer to every question, it is important that you get credit for the ones that you do know. Don't miss any questions through careless mistakes. If at all possible, try to take a second to look back over your answer selection and make sure you've selected the correct answer choice and haven't made a costly careless mistake (such as marking an answer choice that you didn't mean to mark). This quick double check should more than pay for itself in caught mistakes for the time it costs.

Beware of Directly Quoted Answers

Sometimes an answer choice will repeat word for word a portion of the question or reference section. However, beware of such exact duplication – it may be a trap! More than likely, the correct choice will paraphrase or summarize a point, rather than being exactly the same wording.

Slang

Scientific sounding answers are better than slang ones. An answer choice that begins "To compare the outcomes…" is much more likely to be correct than one that begins "Because some people insisted…"

Extreme Statements

Avoid wild answers that throw out highly controversial ideas that are proclaimed as established fact. An answer choice that states the "process should used in certain situations, if…" is much more likely to be correct than one that states the "process should be discontinued completely." The first is a calm rational statement and doesn't even make a definitive, uncompromising stance, using a hedge word "if" to provide wiggle room, whereas the second choice is a radical idea and far more extreme.

Answer Choice Families

When you have two or more answer choices that are direct opposites or parallels, one of them is usually the correct answer. For instance, if one answer choice states "x increases" and another answer choice states "x decreases" or "y increases," then those two or three answer choices are very similar in construction and fall into the same family of answer choices. A family of answer choices is when two or three answer choices are very similar in construction, and yet often have a directly opposite meaning. Usually the correct answer choice will be in that family of answer choices. The "odd man out" or answer choice that doesn't seem to fit the parallel construction of the other answer choices is more likely to be incorrect.

How to Get a Civil Service Job

- Obtain an official announcement and application form from the Federal Government Personnel Office in your local area.

- Complete the application form, as instructed by the announcement. Send the application form and required fee to the Office of Personnel Management whose address will be printed on the application.

- Become familiar with the test through this study guide.

- You will receive by return mail an admission blank for taking the test. (Not all tests require these) The instructions included will list the location and time of the test, and a list of materials that you need to bring to the exam (sharpened pencils, photo id, etc.).

How To Fill Out The Application

The examination announcement will tell you the type of application form required, where to get it and with whom to file it. Once you have the correct form, fill it out carefully, honestly, completely and neatly. Read all parts and fill out all of those that apply to you.

The information you provide must show how you meet any minimum job qualifications in order for you to be eligible to take the test. Therefore, it is important that you answer all questions and provide clear and complete information about your relevant education and experience.

Special reasonable accommodations can be made for people with disabilities to take a test. If you need special accommodations, there is a place on the application where this can be indicated. You must also directly contact the Civil Service agency that announced the examination to describe the accommodations you need. Special arrangements are also available for Sabbath observers, persons on active military duty, and persons taking examinations for more than one Civil Service jurisdiction on the same date.

War Time Disabled Veterans, War Time Veterans, and persons on full-time active duty (other than for training) are eligible for extra credits added to their exam score, if they pass. In most instances, these extra credits can be used only once for any permanent government appointment in New York State. If you want to have the extra credits added to your exam score, you must answer the appropriate questions on the application form. You can waive the extra credits later if you wish. You will be required to produce documentation, such as discharge papers, to prove that you are eligible for the extra credits.

On the application form, there is a place to sign a statement that all the information you have given is accurate. This is your legal affirmation that the statements on your application are true.

To apply for most examinations, you will be required to pay a fee. Information on the amount of the fee and how it can be paid will be found on the announcement. If some applicants are eligible to have the required fee waived, the announcement will explain the requirements for a waiver.

Follow the instructions for submission of your application by the date shown on the announcement. It is advisable to keep a photocopy of your application along with the examination announcement for your records.

Mark the exam date on your calendar

The following information applies specifically to written tests, although some of the information may be helpful in preparing for an oral test or a performance test.

Admission Notices

Approximately a week before the date of the test you will receive an admission notice telling you the date, time and place of the test, and a listing of the examination numbers of the tests you are scheduled to take. You are expected to present this notice at the test center, so be sure to save it. The admission notice tells you if you may or must bring anything with you to the test like a calculator or special equipment.

It also says to bring identification with you to the test center that shows your name, signature and photograph, such as a driver's license or a picture ID. If you have not received an admission notice by the Wednesday before the test or if you lose it, call the state or municipal Civil Service department that announced the examination to find out what to do.

Preparing The Day Before The Test

The day before the test get yourself ready just as you would for any other important appointment. Know where you are going and explore your options for getting there. Check bus or subway connections or get information on where to park ahead of time.

Plan what to take with you to the test. Review your announcement and your admission notice the night before the test to be sure you have everything that you need to bring. Since many tests last three or more hours, you may want to bring a quiet lunch with you. Having a snack or thermos of coffee with you may make you more comfortable during the test. The night before you should consult your admission notice to determine what you will need to take in the morning: Number 2 pencils, a quiet hand-held calculator without keyboard (if allowed), a driver's license or picture ID, your admission notice, watch (to time yourself if you cannot see a clock), and any other required materials.

Get to bed early the night before. Set your alarm clock and allow yourself time to relax. Being rested and having a clear head on the day of the test may help as much as any last minute review.

Also, you should be aware that smoking is NOT allowed at the test center or on the test center grounds.

What To Expect On Test Day

When you leave in the morning, allow extra time to find the room where you will be taking the test and to get yourself settled; however, you will not be allowed into the test centers until one-half hour before your reporting time.

The Test Monitor

There will be a test monitor in the room. The monitor will assure that the tests you are taking are administered fairly to all candidates. On the desk or table you will find the answer sheet you will use for the test, which has directions on how to complete it and a copy of the Candidate Directions. Take the time to familiarize yourself with them while you wait for other candidates to arrive.

The monitor will begin the testing process by giving you some general testing instructions. The monitor will verify your identification, and have you sign your admission notice. The monitor will distribute your test booklets when appropriate, and time your test, announcing and then recording the start time on the chalkboard. The monitor may also give you special oral instructions for your test.

Your monitor will help you if you have a problem. If something goes wrong, if there is a page missing or a misprint or if you have to leave the room, just raise your hand

and the monitor will assist you. If someone else is distracting you, bring it to your monitor's attention. Do not look at the work of other people in the room or you may be disqualified.

When you leave, you must turn in all test materials, even any scrap paper that you may have had during the test. The monitor will collect all your materials before you leave.

The Candidate Directions

Be sure to read the Candidate Directions carefully. The Candidate Directions include information specific to your examination, including the time allowance for the test and if some questions are worth more than others. Unless you are told otherwise, all questions count the same.

There will be explicit directions on determining which questions you are to answer for some tests you do not have to answer every question in every test booklet. But you may have to answer some questions in several test booklets. It is important that you read this portion of the directions VERY carefully. You are responsible for determining which questions you are to answer. The monitor cannot give you specific advice about any test questions, or help you determine the questions you are to answer. That part is up to you.

How To Prepare For The Exam

Commonly people ask, "Will studying help me?" Preparation can significantly improve your chances of doing well on this exam. These are some tips to help you prepare:

- Become aware of the types of questions on the exam:

- Understand the techniques and strategies that will help you on these questions; and
- Practice applying these skills by using the techniques and strategies at home before the exam.

In most cases you will have some time between when you apply for an examination and the date of the test. You can use this time to better prepare yourself for taking the test so that you can do your best on the test date. Once you learn what is on the exam focus your study on specific types of material. Review the basic skills that you need in order to do well.

Make sure that your study time is "quality " time. We suggest uninterrupted blocks of one to two hours. We do not suggest that you study longer than that because shorter, concentrated study periods are proven to be more effective. Your study times must be in a quiet, distraction-free setting that will make your study time more effective. This is very important because concentration is a key to good studying.

Why should you study? These exams are highly competitive and you want every advantage available to do your best!

Studying For A Written Test

Most New York Secretary examinations include a written multiple-choice test. The examination announcement will always provide information on what the test will cover. You can use this information to better prepare yourself to take the test.

The announcement's *Subject of Examination* section will list the areas that the test will cover. As we saw earlier, for the Compensation Claims Clerk examination, the written test will cover three areas, 1) arithmetic computation, 2) arithmetic reasoning, and 3) understanding and interpreting written material.

Sometimes it is apparent by the name of the subject area on what you will be tested. "Arithmetic Computation", for example, would cover simple arithmetic operations like addition, subtraction, multiplication and division. Also, there could be some questions on percents and averages.

Usually, the announcement will contain (or indicate where you can get) an "expanded description" of what will be covered in an area. These paragraph-long descriptions provide additional information on what you will be tested. You should read these sections very carefully, because they provide the best information on what will be covered.

For example, the expanded description for "Arithmetic Reasoning" states: "These questions will test your ability to solve an arithmetic problem presented in sentence or short paragraph form. You must read the problem, understand the situation presented, decide what must be done to solve it, and apply the appropriate arithmetic operation (s) in the appropriate order, in order to determine the correct answer. Knowledge of addition, subtraction, multiplication, and division will be necessary. Questions may also involve the use of percents, decimals, and fractions."

This information provides a clearer picture of the type of mathematical questions that you will see on the test.

There are certain words that appear often in the names and descriptions of the areas that will be covered by the examination:

- principles, practices, procedures, methods, techniques

- understanding, interpreting, applying, reasoning, solving

The first set of words is usually a sign that you will be asked about your *knowledge* of a given subject. The second set of words usually indicates that you will be tested for a *skill* or *ability*. You would prepare differently for a test of knowledge than for a test of a skill or ability.

Most secretary jobs are considered Clerk/Typist or stenographer. In order to be considered for these jobs you will need to pass the Verbal, Clerical, Typing and Stenography portions of the Civil Service test. You also need to be a high school graduate or have 6 months of appropriate experience to be rated GS-2 Clerk/Typist or GS-3 Stenographer, to be rated GS-3 Clerk/Typist, GS-4 Stenographer you will need 1 year of appropriate experience or 1 year of post-high school education.

Verbal Abilities Test

This test includes questions that measure language skills such as knowledge of the meaning of words, relationships of words, ability to spell common words, and recognition of sentences that are grammatically correct. It also includes questions that measure your ability to read and understand written material. There are 85 questions with a time limit of 35 minutes. This portion of the test is broken down like this:

- Word meaning   25 questions
- Analogy   20 questions
- Grammar   10 questions
- Spelling   20 questions
- Reading   10 questions

The question types are in no particular order; they will be mixed throughout the 85 questions. You will have 5 word meaning, then 4 analogy, then 2 grammar, then 4 spelling, and then 2 reading questions. This series repeats 4 times. Each question has equal value for your score. Your score is the number of questions you answer correctly so try to answer all questions. You will not be penalized for an incorrect answer.

Verbal Abilities Tips

Secret 1 You can mark in the test booklet

Remember that you can mark in your test booklet. Some people find it very helpful to underline key words and cross out obviously incorrect answers. Also writing in your test booklet can help you stay focused on the task at hand. It will help you isolate the correct choices.

Secret 2 Answer the easier questions first

All of the questions count as the same for your score. Sometimes people don't get to the easier questions because they spend too much time on the ones that are more difficult for them. This is a timed test and you must remember to use your time wisely.

To achieve the highest number of correct answers we suggest that you attempt the first question. If you can answer it quickly and easily then do so. Work the problem and mark the answer in the question booklet, then mark the correct answer on the answer sheet.

It the question seems too difficult circle the question number in the question booklet. Make a guess and go ahead and mark that guess on your answer sheet. Remember there is no penalty for a wrong guess and a wrong answer is as good as no answer. If you have time later you can go back over your question booklet and try to redo any questions in the section that you are working on to see if you can get an answer that you are more comfortable with.

If you see a question that seems to be taking too much time put a mark beside it and come back to it later. Mark an answer on the answer sheet in case you don't have enough time to come back to it. Make sure that you don't leave any questions on the answer sheet blank. There is NO penalty for guessing. You should use all of the allotted time as effectively as possible.

Grammar

Choose which of four ways of writing the underlined part of the sentence is correct.

<u>As a consumer, one can accept</u> the goods offered to us or we can reject them, but we cannot determine their quality or change the system's priorities.

A. NO CHANGE

B. We the consumer either can accept

C. The consumer can accept

D. As consumers, we can accept

Let's look at a couple of different methods and steps to solving this problem.

1. Agreement in Pronoun Number

All pronouns have to agree in number to their antecedent or noun that they are representing. In the underlined portion, the pronoun "one" has as its antecedent the noun "consumer".

Go through and match up each of the pronouns in the answer choices with their antecedents.

A. consumer, one – correctly matches singular antecedent to singular pronoun

B. We, consumer – incorrectly matches plural antecedent to singular pronoun

C. consumer – no pronoun

D. consumers, we – correctly matches plural antecedent to plural pronoun

Based on pronoun number agreement, you can eliminate choice B from consideration because it fails the test.

2. Parallelism

Not only do the pronouns and antecedents in the underlined portion of the sentence have to be correct, but the rest of the sentence has to match as well. The remainder of the sentence has to be parallel to the underlined portion. In part of the sentence that is not underlined is the phrase "we can reject them," and another phrase, "but we cannot determine." Notice how both of these phrases use the plural pronoun "we". This means that the underlined portion of the sentence has to agree with the rest of the sentence and have matching plural pronouns and nouns as well.

Quickly review the answer choices and look for whether the nouns and pronouns in the answer choices are singular or plural.

A. consumer, one – singular noun and singular pronoun

B. We, consumer – plural pronoun and singular noun

C. consumer – singular noun

D. consumers, we – plural noun and plural pronoun

Only choice D has both a plural noun and a plural pronoun, making choice D correct.

Reading

Skimming

Your first task when you begin reading is to answer the question "What is the topic of the selection?" This can best be answered by quickly skimming the passage for the general idea, stopping to read only the first sentence of each paragraph. A paragraph's first is usually the main topic sentence, and it gives you a summary of the content of the paragraph.

Once you've skimmed the passage, stopping to read only the first sentences, you will have a general idea about what it is about, as well as what is the expected topic in each paragraph.

Each question will contain clues as to where to find the answer in the passage. Do not just randomly search through the passage for the correct answer to each question. Search scientifically. Find key word(s) or ideas in the question that are going to either contain or be near the correct answer. These are typically nouns, verbs, numbers, or phrases in the question that will probably be duplicated in the passage. Once you have identified those key word(s) or idea, skim the passage quickly to find where those key word(s) or idea appears. The correct answer choice will be nearby.

Example: What caused Martin to suddenly return to Paris?

The key word is Paris. Skim the passage quickly to find where this word appears. The answer will be close by that word.
However, sometimes key words in the question are not repeated in the passage. In those cases, search for the general idea of the question.

Example: Which of the following was the psychological impact of the author's childhood upon the remainder of his life?

Key words are "childhood" or "psychology". While searching for those words, be alert for other words or phrases that have similar meaning, such as "emotional effect" or "mentally" which could be used in the passage, rather than the exact word "psychology".

Numbers or years can be particularly good key words to skim for, as they stand out from the rest of the text.

Example: Which of the following best describes the influence of Monet's work in the 20th century?

20th contains numbers and will easily stand out from the rest of the text. Use 20th as the key word to skim for in the passage.

Other good key word(s) may be in quotation marks. These identify a word or phrase that is copied directly from the passage. In those cases, the word(s) in quotation marks are exactly duplicated in the passage.

Example: In her college years, what was meant by Margaret's "drive for excellence"?

"Drive for excellence" is a direct quote from the passage and should be easy to find. Once you've quickly found the correct section of the passage to find the answer, focus upon the answer choices. Sometimes a choice will repeat word for word a portion of the passage near the answer. However, beware of such duplication – it may be a trap! More than likely, the correct choice will paraphrase or summarize the related portion of the passage, rather than being exactly the same wording.

For the answers that you think are correct, read them carefully and make sure that they answer the question. An answer can be factually correct, but it MUST answer the question asked. Additionally, two answers can both be seemingly correct, so be sure to read all of the answer choices, and make sure that you get the one that BEST answers the question.

Some questions will not have a key word.

Example: Which of the following would the author of this passage likely agree with?

In these cases, look for key words in the answer choices. Then skim the passage to find where the answer choice occurs. By skimming to find where to look, you can minimize the time required.

Sometimes it may be difficult to identify a good key word in the question to skim for in the passage. In those cases, look for a key word in one of the answer choices to skim for. Often the answer choices can all be found in the same paragraph, which can quickly narrow your search.

Paragraph Focus

Focus upon the first sentence of each paragraph, which is the most important. The main topic of the paragraph is usually there.
Once you've read the first sentence in the paragraph, you have a general idea about what each paragraph will be about. As you read the questions, try to determine which paragraph will have the answer. Paragraphs have a concise topic. The answer should either obviously be there or obviously not. It will save time if you can jump straight to the paragraph, so try to remember what you learned from the first sentences.

Example: The first paragraph is about poets; the second is about poetry. If a question asks about poetry, where will the answer be? The second paragraph.

The main idea of a passage is typically spread across all or most of its paragraphs. Whereas the main idea of a paragraph may be completely different than the main idea of the very next paragraph, a main idea for a passage affects all of the paragraphs in one form or another.

Example: What is the main idea of the passage?

For each answer choice, try to see how many paragraphs are related. It can help to count how many sentences are affected by each choice, but it is best to see how many paragraphs are affected by the choice. Typically the answer choices will include incorrect choices that are main ideas of individual paragraphs, but not the entire passage. That is why it is crucial to choose ideas that are supported by the most paragraphs possible.

Eliminate Choices

Some choices can quickly be eliminated. "Andy Warhol lived there." Is Andy Warhol even mentioned in the article? If not, quickly eliminate it.
choice. If the reference exists, scratch it off as a choice. Similar choices may be crossed off simultaneously if they are close enough.

In choices that ask you to choose "which answer choice does NOT describe?" or "all of the following answer choices are identifiable characteristics, EXCEPT which?" look for answers that are similarly worded. Since only one answer can be correct, if there are two answers that appear to mean the same thing, they must BOTH be incorrect, and can be eliminated.

Example Answer Choices:

A.)   changing values and attitudes

B.)   a large population of mobile or uprooted people

These answer choices are similar; they both describe a fluid culture. Because of their similarity, they can be linked together. Since the answer can have only one choice, they can also be eliminated together.

When presented with a question that offers two choices, or neither choice, or both choice, it is rarely both choices.

Example: When an atom emits a beta particle, the mass of the atom will:

A.   increase

B.   decrease.

C.   stay the same.

D.   either increase or decrease depending on conditions.

Answer D will rarely be correct, the answers are usually more concrete.

Contextual Clues

Look for contextual clues. An answer can be right but not correct. The contextual clues will help you find the answer that is most right and is correct. Understand the context in which a phrase is stated.

When asked for the implied meaning of a statement made in the passage, immediately go find the statement and read the context it was made in. Also, look for an answer choice that has a similar phrase to the statement in question.

Example: In the passage, what is implied by the phrase "Churches have become more or less part of the furniture"?

Find an answer choice that is similar or describes the phrase "part of the furniture" as that is the key phrase in the question. "Part of the furniture" is a saying that means something is fixed, immovable, or set in their ways. Those are all similar ways of saying "part of the furniture." As such, the correct answer choice will probably include a similar rewording of the expression.

Example: Why was John described as "morally desperate".

The answer will probably have some sort of definition of morals in it. "Morals" refers to a code of right and wrong behavior, so the correct answer choice will likely have words that mean something like that.

Time Management

In technical passages, do not get lost on the technical terms. Skip them and move on. You want a general understanding of what is going on, not a mastery of the passage.

When you encounter material in the selection that seems difficult to understand, bracket it. It often may not be necessary and can be skipped. Only spend time trying to understand it if it is going to be relevant for a question. Understand difficult phrases only as a last resort.

Answer general questions before detail questions. A reader with a good understanding of the whole passage can often answer general questions without rereading a word. Get the easier questions out of the way before tackling the more time consuming ones.

Identify each question by type. Usually the wording of a question will tell you whether you can find the answer by referring directly to the passage or by using your reasoning powers. You alone know which question types you customarily handle with ease and which give you trouble and will require more time. Save the difficult questions for last.

Warnings

When asked for a conclusion that may be drawn, look for critical "hedge" phrases, such as likely, may, can, will often, sometimes, etc, often, almost, mostly, usually, generally, rarely, sometimes. Question writers insert these hedge phrases, to cover every possibility. Often an answer will be wrong simply because it leaves no room for exception.

Example: Animals live longer in cold places than animals in warm places.

This answer choice is wrong, because there are exceptions in which certain warm climate animals live longer. This answer choice leaves no possibility of exception. It states that every animal species in cold places live longer than animal species in warm places. Correct answer choices will typically have a key hedge word to leave room for exceptions.

Example: In severe cold, a polar bear cub is likely to survive longer than an adult polar bear.

This answer choice is correct, because not only does the passage imply that younger animals survive better in the cold, it also allows for exceptions to exist.
The use of the word "likely" leaves room for cases in which a polar bear cub might not survive longer than the adult polar bear.

When asked how a word is used in the passage, don't use your existing knowledge of the word. The question is being asked precisely because there is some strange or unusual usage of the word in the passage. Go to the passage and use contextual clues to determine the answer. Don't simply use the popular definition you already know.

Stay alert for "switchbacks". These are the words and phrases frequently used to alert you to shifts in thought. The most common switchback word is "but". Others include although, however, nevertheless, on the other hand, even though, while, in spite of, despite, regardless of.

Once you know which paragraph the answer will be in, focus on that paragraph. However, don't get distracted by a choice that is factually true about the paragraph. Your search is for the answer that answers the question, which may be about a tiny aspect in the paragraph. Stay focused and don't fall for an answer that describes the larger picture of the paragraph. Always go back to the question and make sure you're choosing an answer that actually answers the question and is not just a true statement.

Sample Question from the Reading Test:

Mark Twain was well aware of his celebrity. He was among the first authors to employ a clipping service to track press coverage of himself, and it was not unusual for him to issue his own press statements if he wanted to influence or "spin" coverage of a particular story. The celebrity Twain achieved during his last ten years still reverberates today. Nearly all of his most popular novels were published before 1890, long before his hair grayed or he began to wear his famous white suit in public. We appreciate the author but seem to remember the celebrity.

Based on the passage above, Mark Twain seemed interested in:

    A. maintaining his celebrity
    B. selling more of his books
    C. hiding his private life
    D. gaining popularity

Let's look at a couple of different methods of solving this problem.

1. Identify the key words in each answer choice. These are the nouns and verbs that are the most important words in the answer choice.

A. maintaining, celebrity
B. selling, books
C. hiding, life
D. gaining, popularity

Now try to match up each of the key words with the passage and see where they fit. You're trying to find synonyms and/or exact replication between the key words in the answer choices and key words in the passage.

A. maintaining – no matches; celebrity – matches in sentences 1, 3, and 5

B. selling – no matches; books – matches with "novels" in sentence 4.

C. hiding – no matches; life – no matches

D. gaining – no matches; popularity –matches with "celebrity" in sentences 1, 3, and
    5, because they can be synonyms

At this point there are only two choices that have more than one match, choices A and D, and they both have the same number of matches, and with the same word in the passage, which is the word "celebrity" in the passage. This is a good sign, because the exam writers will often write two answer choices that are close. Having two answer choices pointing towards the same key word is a strong indicator that those key words hold the "key" to finding the right answer.

Now let's compare choice A and D and the unmatched key words. Choice A still has "maintaining" which doesn't have a clear match, while choice D has "gaining" which doesn't have a clear match. While neither of those have clear matches in the passage, ask yourself what are the best arguments that would support any kind of connection with either of those two words.

"Maintaining" makes sense when you consider that Twain was interested in tracking his press coverage and that he was actively managing the "spin" of certain stories.

"Gaining" makes sense when you consider that Twain was actively issuing his own press releases, however one key point to remember is that he was only issuing these press releases after another story was already in existence.

Since Twain's press releases were not being released in a news vacuum, but rather as a response mechanism to ensure control over the angle of a story, his releases were more to *maintain* control over his image, rather than *gain* an image in the first place.

Furthermore, when comparing the terms "popularity" and "celebrity", there are similarities between the words, but in referring back to the passage, it is clear that "celebrity" has a stronger connection to the passage, being the exact word used three times in the passage.

Since "celebrity" has a stronger match than "popularity" and "maintaining" makes more sense than "gaining," it is clear that choice A is correct.

2. Use a process of elimination.

A. maintaining his celebrity – The passage discusses how Mark Twain was both aware of his celebrity status and would take steps to ensure that he got the proper coverage in any news story and maintained the image he desired. This is the correct answer.

B. selling more of his books – Mark Twain's novels are mentioned for their popularity and while common sense would dictate that he would be interested in selling more of his books, the passage makes no mention of him doing anything to promote sales.

C. hiding his private life – While the passage demonstrates that Mark Twain was keenly interested in how the public viewed his life, it does not indicate that he cared about hiding his private life, not even mentioning his life outside of the public eye. The passage deals with how he was seen by the public.

D. gaining popularity – At first, this sounds like a good answer choice, because Mark Twain's popularity is mentioned several times. The main difference though is that he wasn't trying to gain popularity, but simply ensuring that the popularity he had was not distorted by bad press.

Verbal Abilities Sample Questions

Word Meaning:

To verify means most nearly

A) figure   C) explain

B) guarantee   D) confirm

The definition of verify is to prove or confirm so the correct answer is D.

Analogies:

Research is related to Findings as Training is related to

A) exams   C) supervision

B) skill   D) understanding

The second word is the intended result of the first word. The correct answer is B.

Grammar:

A) The people which has guarantees these products are responsible.

B) These products can be depended on, for their truth has been guaranteed by reliable persons.

C) Reliable persons guarantee the facts with regards to the truth of these statements.

D) Most all these products have been supported by persons who are reliable and can be depended upon.

D – reliable and can be depended upon is repetitious. A – which should be who.   C - the facts with regards to the truth is repetitious and awkward. The correct answer is B.

Spelling:

A) receve

B) recieve

C) receive

D) none of these

The correct answer is C.

Reading:

Those who have difficulty reading are usually those who have not read much. The habit of reading is probably instilled during childhood; those children with parents who like to read also tend to acquire a fondness for books. Adults who have never learned to appreciate reading are likely to avoid it.

The paragraph best supports the statement that those who have avoided reading during childhood:

A)   will probably not find reading easier as they get older.

B)   will transmit a hateful attitude toward books to their children.

C)   were probably kept from reading by their parents.

D)   did so only because interesting reading material was made available by their parents.

The correct answer is A. Each of the other choices makes assumptions about parents that are not expressed or implied in the paragraph.

Clerical Abilities Test

This portion of the exam is a test of speed and accuracy on 4 clerical tasks. There are 120 questions with a time limit of 15 minutes. The categories are:

- Name and number checking 30 questions
- Alphabetical order   30 questions
- Arithmetic   30 questions
- Letters and numbers   30 questions

The questions in this section are in no particular order. There are 5 questions of each type repeated, until they total 120 questions. On this section you are penalized for incorrect answers, unlike the verbal abilities test, where you are not.

You will have 10 minutes to study the directions and sample questions that are provided. You will be told when to begin the actual test which only lasts 15 minutes.

Reread the secrets and strategies already listed in this booklet so that you can apply them to this section. Remember there is one BIG difference on this portion you are penalized for incorrect answers.

Scoring the Clerical Abilities Section

Your score on this portion is determined by the number of right answers minus ¼ of the number of wrong answers. Questions left blank are given neither plus nor minus credit. Every filled-in but incorrect answer lowers your score slightly. If you answer 90 questions correctly, 20 incorrectly, and leave 10 unanswered, you will receive 90 points for your correct answers, minus 5 points for your incorrect answers (1/4 x 20), for a total score of 85 points. Your final score is 5 points lower because of the 20 wrong answers. It is not to your benefit to guess blindly on this portion.

Clerical Abilities Sample Questions

Alike or Different

Tip 1

Make sure you understand and memorize what each answer choice indicates. Try to not keep looking back and forth from the questions to the directions for each question. This will cost you time if you have to do this.

Tip 2

When trying to answer the questions that are numbers try to read them as you would a phone number. Three digits followed by four digits. This will help as you compare them to see if the first three digits are the same and if they are, are the last four the same? Watch out for reversals though memorize "first three, then four" for example; be able to tell the difference in 4326787 and 4623787.

Tip 3

When trying to answer the questions that involve names try to separate them into categories such as first name, initials, then last names. This may be helpful if broken down into these categories to compare. Watch out for "double letters" in one name which is a single letter in another. For example, Charles Randell and Charles Randel. Another key is to watch out for "silent letters". For example, Kelley O'Connor and Kelly O' Connor. Be careful to look for "look-alike letters" such as "s" and "z" or "m" and "n". For example, Michael Ellenberger and Michael Ellemberger.

Watch out for "letter reversals" such as "d" and "b", or "p" and "q." Example: Derek Dodson, and Derek Dobson. Our last warning for this section is to be careful of different common spellings. For example; Francis Morrison, and Frances Morrison.

Compare the three names or numbers and mark the answer –

A if ALL THREE names or numbers are exactly ALIKE

B if only the FIRST and SECOND names or numbers are exactly ALIKE

C if only the FIRST and THIRD names or numbers are exactly ALIKE

D if only the SECOND and THIRD names or numbers are exactly ALIKE

E if ALL THREE names or numbers are DIFFERENT

1.   3457988   3457986   3457986

The correct answer is D.

In this section it would help if you could learn what A, B, C, D, and E stand for.

Alphabetizing

Tip 1

Alphabetize by the first letter of the last name. If two or more last names begin with the same letter, look to the second letter in this name. If the first two letters of the last name are the same, go to the third letter, then fourth, etc. If the letters in the last names are identical, but one name is longer, the shorter name goes first because it "runs out of letters." For example Smyth comes before Smythe. Lowercase letters, apostrophes and hyphens in names shouldn't confuse you. Apply the rules that have already been stated.

Tip 2

If the last names are exactly the same look at the first name or first initial and then alphabetize using the first letter of the first name. If the first name begins with the same letter look to the second letter. If the first name is just an initial that initial will come before the first name beginning with that same letter, for example; Holley, R. comes before Holley, Russell. Even if there is a middle name after the first initial or two initials a first initial will always precede a full first name, Holley, R. Thomas before Holley Russell. Alphabetical rules still apply.

Tip 3

If the first names or initials are exactly the same, look to the middle initial or middle name and follow the same rules that have been stated already.

Find the correct place for this name:
DeMattia, Jessica

  A) →
     DeLong, Jesse
  B) →
     DeMatteo, Jessie
  C) →
     Derby, Jessie S.
  D) →
     Deshazo, L. M.
  E) →

The correct answer is C. DeMatteo, Jessie
                              DeMattia, Jessica
                           Derby, Jessie S.

Arithmetic

Tip 1

Be familiar with basic mathematical skills such as addition, subtraction, multiplication, and division. In addition know how to "carry." If the ones column goes over 9 you must "carry" the digit to the tens column. For example if the question is: 28 + 13 = ? 8 + 3 = 11 so you place a "1" in the ones column and "carry" a "1" to the tens column and add 1 + 2 + 1, so the answer is "41."

With subtraction you must remember to "borrow". For example in the question 13 – 8 = ?, it is not possible in the one's column to subtract 3 – 8. Therefore, you must borrow the 1 (which means 10) from the tens column and subtract 13 – 8 = 5. When you are using larger numbers, such as 33 – 8 = ?, you still borrow "10" from

- 53 -

the tens column, but since you have used one ten in the ones column you only have 2 left in the tens column which is now "20".

To answer multiplication questions you must be familiar with basic multiplication "times tables". Also remember to "carry" as you do in addition.

When answering division questions you will need to be familiar with basic division skills and be able to do simple "long division." One way to quickly check your answer is to multiply the problem back out afterwards to make sure that you have the correct numerals.

Tip 2

Review all basic addition, subtraction, multiplication, and division facts weeks prior to taking the exam. If you find a weakness in your skills make sure to practice that particular set of facts until you are completely comfortable with them. You do not want simple facts that can be memorized to slow you down when you are taking the exam. Practice and practice these facts to increase your speed and accuracy.

Tip 3

Even though "add," "subtract," "multiply," and "divide" are printed above each question make sure that you also look for the "sign" (+, -, x, /) in the actual problem. It is easy to make a careless error when answering mathematical problems so double-checking the word – add with the sign - +, will give you some assurance that you are working the problem correctly.

Tip 4

Each of the mathematical problems will have numerical answers for A, B, C, and D, but answer E is always "none of these." If the answer you found is not listed remember to choose E.

Subtract:
```
  68
- 47
```

A) 10   B)22
C)20   D)11
E) none of these

The correct answer is E, none of these (21).

Letters and Numbers

Tip 1

These questions are designed to test your observation skills. You will be given five sets of letters and numbers (four of each), followed by five suggested answers, A, B, C, D, and E which is always "none of these."

For each number question you will find which of the suggested answers contains letters and numbers. You must find the answer which contains numbers and letters that are all in the question. Only ONE suggested answer will be correct for each question.

Find which one of the suggested answers appears in that question.

    1.   Z 6 5 V 9 3 9 N

A=3, 8, K, N
B=5, 8, N, V
C=3, 9, V, Z
D=5, 9, K, Z
E=none of these

The correct answer is C.

Typing Test

In this test, the applicant meets a single task, copying material exactly as it is presented. You must demonstrate how rapidly you can do so and with what accuracy.

The typing portion is used at the hiring agencies discretion. The employer may use the Civil Service typing test or another at their own discretion.

In the usual typewriter examination procedure, each applicant is given a copy of the test and two sheets of typewriter paper. The test takes about 15 minutes to complete.

Three minutes are allowed to read the instructions on the face of the test and three minutes for practice typing. The practice element consists of typing instructions for spacing, capitalization, etc., and warns that any erasures will be penalized. This practice portion also assures that the typewriter is performing properly.

After the three minutes of practice the applicants put fresh paper in their typewriter and turn the test page over and read the test for two minutes. After the two minutes you will be instructed to start typing. Five minutes are allowed for the actual typing.

You must type the complete section about once to meet the speed requirement of 40 words a minute. If this is not attained, the test is not scored for accuracy.

The basic principles in charging typing errors are:

Charge 1 word for each –

- Word or punctuation mark incorrectly typed or in which there is an erasure.
- Series of consecutive words omitted, repeated, inserted, transposed, or erased. There is a charge for errors within the series but the total charge cannot exceed the number of words.

- Line or part of a line typed over other material, typed with all capitals, or typed with the fingers on the wrong keys.
- Change from the margin where most lines begun by you or from the paragraph indention use most frequently use.

The typing score in the official examination reflects both speed and accuracy, with accuracy weighted twice as heavily as speed.

Tip 1

Be careful of the most common errors. Don't strike one letter for another. Common errors in this category include; "r" for "t," or "t" for "r." Other common letter switches are; Hitting "i" for "o," "a" for "s," "I" for "e," and "m" for "n." Reversals for all of the above also happen.

Tip 2

Be careful that you don't transpose letters. Common examples of typing letters in reverse order are; "re" instead of "er," "op" instead of "po," "ew" instead of "we," "oi" instead of "io," and lastly "to" instead of "ot." If you find these errors in your work, practice hitting those letters in the correct order.

Tip 3

Be cautious of incorrect hand alignment, weakness in the smaller fingers, and reading too far ahead may cause omitted-letter errors. If you find that you are missing letters after typing your work these three areas are the ones that you need to work on.

Sample typing passage:

Canada emerged from World War II a much stronger country, and a more independent one. Its major problem has been that of trying to keep the nation together. In French-speaking Quebec, there is a movement to try to set up a separate nation.

There are many common postwar problems in Latin America. With some exceptions, as in Mexico, these countries are dominated by dictators who usually have the support of the military. There are many pressures on Latin American governments. Mostly, they involve the great gap that exists between the very rich and the very poor. In most countries of Latin America, there are also great differences in wealth between the cities and the countryside. Despite the slums of the larger cities, the urban areas continue to lure people from the farms. People hope to find jobs in the cities and to make more money than they can on the farms. Inflation is a threat to most of the countries of Latin America, where the price of food, clothing, and shelter can, in some cases, double each year.

The newly discovered oil resources of Mexico make that country especially important to the United States. Mexico and other Latin American countries do not trust the United States.

Table of Speed vs. Accuracy

Gross Words Per Minute	GS-2, GS-3, GS-4 Clerk - Typist GS-3, GS-4, GS-5, Clerk - Stenographer
Under 40	Ineligible
40	3
41-42	4
43-44	5
45-47	6
48-49	6
50-52	7
53-54	7
55-56	8
57-59	8
60-61	9
62-64	9
65-66	10
67-68	10
69-71	11
72-73	11
74-76	12
77-78	12
79-80	12

Dictation Test

This is part of the Civil Service Stenographer-Typist Examination. This portion includes a practice dictation and a test exercise, each consisting of 240 words. The rate of dictation is 80 words per minute.

This test differs from a conventional dictation test in the method of transcribing notes. You are not require to type a transcript of the notes, but to follow a procedure that permits machine scoring of the test.

The transcript booklet gives the stenographer parts of the dictated passage, but leaves blank spaces where many of the words belong. With adequate notes the stenographer can easily fit the correct words into the blank spaces, which are numbered 1-125. To the left of the printed partial transcript you will find a list of words, each word denoted A, B, C, or D beside it. None of the words in the list are marked E because the answer E is reserved for any question when the word dictated for that spot does not appear in the list.

Sample dictation passage:

The US East Coast struggled to break through massive snowdrifts and restore main transport links Tuesday after the worst winter storm in a decade, as officials warned it could take at least another day for life to return to normal.

Traffic still crawled along in cities from Washington and Baltimore to Philadelphia, New York and Boston. Schools and most government agencies were closed as plows cleared main roads, lining the streets with mountainous snow banks. Airports reopened in Washington and New York to lengthy lines of passengers who have been stranded since Sunday, and the backlog wasn't expected to be cleared at least until Wednesday.

Subway trains resumed service in Washington, though they passed less frequently than usual. Buses splashed through the slush on main roads, but they were few and far between.

Many residential streets remained impassable, and cars were buried beneath piles of snow pushed aside by the plows.

The snowfall -- one of the heaviest recorded in many cities -- began before dawn Sunday, triggering states of emergency in Delaware, Kentucky, Maryland, New Jersey, New York, Pennsylvania, Virginia, West Virginia and the city of Washington.

The most impressive snowfalls came in the central Appalachian Mountains, with 1.24 meters (49 inches) recorded in western Maryland and 1.01 meters (40 inches) in western Pennsylvania.

Washington's 255 plows were plying the streets with salt, as Mayor Anthony Williams, who cut short a four-day vacation in Puerto Rico to return to the snow-bound US capital, said it would take several days to clear the mess.

Word Bank

after—A
agencies—A
along—D
another—B
Anthony—C
Appalacian—A
as—C

banks—B
beneath—A
break—B
buried—D

cities—C
clear—A
cleared—D
closed—B
could—B

lengthy--B
life—A
lines—A
lining--C
links--B

main--C
massive--D
most--B

normal--A

officials--B

plows--A

return--A
roads--C

crawled—C
cut—A

day—C
days—D
decade—B

east—A

far—D
few—B
for—C

government—C

in—D

least—B

snow--C
snowdrifts--A
snowfalls--B
still--B
streets--C

take--D
through--D
transport--A

warned--D
western--C
who--B
winter--B
worst--C

The US East Coast struggled to __(1)__ through ___(2)___ ___(3)___ and restore main___(4)___ __(5)__ Tuesday __(6)__ the __(7)__ __(8)__ storm in a decade, _(9)_ officials __(10)__ it could take at __(11)__ __(12)__ __(13)_ for life to __(14)__ to normal.

* This is a sample passage with blanks for you to practice with. Get someone to read the dictation to you and then try to answer or fill in the blanks. This is a very short sample. On the actual transcript you will fill in 120 words. Remember if you do not see the correct word use the letter E which means that the word does not appear in the word bank.

Special Report: Exams and Positions Available

I. The following tests are used mostly for new hiring:

SERIES 6500 - Clerical Office & Administrative Support Test (COAST)

This test is used to fill non-typing clerical jobs such as Clerk 1, 2, 3 and 4; Accounting Clerk and Caseworker Assistant.

SERIES 1333 - Professional Entry Test (PET) This test is used to fill professional jobs such as Medicaid analyst, probation and parole officer, computer programmer, purchasing agent, and human resource analyst.

SERIES 4444 - Typing Careers Test *** This test is used to fill jobs such as Typist Clerk 1, 2 or 3; Secretary; and Word Processor Operator. There is a typing skills test - you must type at least 40 wpm to pass - and a multiple choice written test.

SERIES 1050 - Group Benefits Claims Assistant

Special Report: Civil Service Experience and Training Ratings

Many state jobs require applicants to compete on written exams. But for some jobs, instead of being given a written exam, applicants are graded on their prior experience, education and/or training. Such Experience & Training Ratings, or "E&T's", are generally used for jobs which require applicants to have prior experience in a specific field.

Experience & Training Ratings compare applicant experience to the duties of the job applied for. Generally, the more experience an applicant has had in jobs like the one applied for, the higher the rating will be. Consideration is given to the type of work, its complexity, the applicant's level of responsibility, supervisory control, etc. For some jobs, the recency of the experience may also be a consideration. (For example, in the computer field, recency of experience can be an important factor.) In addition to experience, applicant education may be rated. Again, the more specifically relevant an applicant's experience is to the job applied for, the higher the rating will be.

When Experience & Training Ratings are used, the evaluations are based on the applicants' experience and education as they describe it on the official state pre-employment application form (SF-10). Final grades based on the E&T Rating range from a low of 70 to a high of 99. Grade results are mailed to applicants a few weeks after we receive the application.

Special Report: Sample Questions

Many state jobs require skill in analyzing, understanding, and interpreting written material of varying levels of difficulty. The reading comprehension questions on our tests are designed to measure applicants' abilities to understand and interpret written material. These questions require an employee to read and understand a paragraph, and then, to choose an answer based on their understanding of the main concept put forth in the written passage. The correct answer will usually restate this main concept, using different wording. In some cases, the correct answer will be a conclusion that is drawn from the content of the paragraph. After reading the passage, choose as your answer the statement that is best supported by the contents of the passage.

Paragraph 1. A viable affirmative action program must contain specific procedures designed to achieve equal employment opportunities for specified groups. Appropriate procedures, without necessary determination to carry them out, are useless. Determination, without well defined procedures, will achieve only partial success.

The paragraph best supports the statement that:

1. Well defined procedures will assure the success of an affirmative action program.
2. A high degree of determination is necessary and sufficient for a highly successful affirmative action program.
3. It is impossible for an agency to develop a viable affirmative action program.
4. An agency may guarantee success of its affirmative action program by developing and implementing well defined procedures.
5. Two important ingredients of a successful affirmative action program are well defined procedures and a sincere resolve to implement those procedures.

Paragraph 2. Claimants who have become unemployed by voluntarily leaving the job, by refusing to accept suitable work, or due to misconduct should be temporarily disqualified from receiving benefits. However, the disqualification period should never be longer than the average period required for a worker to find employment. Unemployment insurance is designed to alleviate hardship due to unemployment. Benefits should definitely be paid if unemployment continues beyond a certain point and the claimant can show that he has made an honest effort to find employment.

The paragraph best supports the statement that:

1. If a claimant cannot find work after a certain period of time, he/she should no longer receive benefits.
2. In cases of willful misconduct, disqualification should continue indefinitely.
3. The reasons for unemployment change as the period of unemployment gets longer.
4. If a claimant cannot find employment after a certain period of time, he/she should be allowed to receive unemployment insurance benefits.
5. If a claimant chooses voluntary unemployment, he/she should receive unemployment insurance benefits immediately.

Reading Comprehension Sample Question Answers and Explanations

1. The correct alternative, 5, restates the idea presented in the paragraph. Statements 1 and 2 each contain only one of the ingredients. Alternative 4 overstates the implications of the paragraph.

2. The correct alternative, 4, summarizes the meaning of the passage as a whole. Alternative 1 concerns the length of time the claimant should receive benefits. Alternatives 2 and 5 contradict parts of the passage and the idea expressed in 3 is not addressed in the paragraph.

Special Report: What Your Test Score Will Tell You About Your IQ

Did you know that most standardized tests correlate very strongly with IQ? In fact, your general intelligence is a better predictor of your success than any other factor, and most tests intentionally measure this trait to some degree to ensure that those selected by the test are truly qualified for the test's purposes.

Before we can delve into the relation between your test score and IQ, I will first have to explain what exactly is IQ. Here's the formula:

Your IQ = 100 + (Number of standard deviations below or above the average)*15

Now, let's define standard deviations by using an example. If we have 5 people with 5 different heights, then first we calculate the average. Let's say the average was 65 inches. The standard deviation is the "average distance" away from the average of each of the members. It is a direct measure of variability - if the 5 people included Jackie Chan and Shaquille O'Neal, obviously there's a lot more variability in that group than a group of 5 sisters who are all within 6 inches in height of each other. The standard deviation uses a number to characterize the average range of difference within a group.

A convenient feature of most groups is that they have a "normal" distribution-makes sense that most things would be normal, right? Without getting into a bunch of statistical mumbo-jumbo, you just need to know that if you know the average of the group and the standard deviation, you can successfully predict someone's percentile rank in the group.

Confused? Let me give you an example. If instead of 5 people's heights, we had 100 people, we could figure out their rank in height JUST by knowing the average, standard deviation, and their height. We wouldn't need to know each person's height and manually rank them, we could just predict their rank based on three numbers.

What this means is that you can take your PERCENTILE rank that is often given with your test and relate this to your RELATIVE IQ of people taking the test - that is, your IQ relative to the people taking the test. Obviously, there's no way to know your actual IQ because the people taking a standardized test are usually not very good samples of the general population- many of those with extremely low IQ's never achieve a level of success or competency necessary to complete a typical standardized test. In fact, professional psychologists who measure IQ actually have to use non-written tests that can fairly measure the IQ of those not able to complete a traditional test.

The bottom line is to not take your test score too seriously, but it is fun to compute your "relative IQ" among the people who took the test with you. I've done the calculations below. Just look up your percentile rank in the left and then you'll see your "relative IQ" for your test in the right hand column-

Percentile Rank	Your Relative IQ		Percentile Rank	Your Relative IQ
99	135		59	103
98	131		58	103
97	128		57	103
96	126		56	102
95	125		55	102
94	123		54	102
93	122		53	101
92	121		52	101
91	120		51	100
90	119		50	100
89	118		49	100
88	118		48	99
87	117		47	99
86	116		46	98
85	116		45	98
84	115		44	98
83	114		43	97
82	114		42	97
81	113		41	97
80	113		40	96
79	112		39	96
78	112		38	95
77	111		37	95
76	111		36	95
75	110		35	94
74	110		34	94
73	109		33	93
72	109		32	93
71	108		31	93
70	108		30	92
69	107		29	92
68	107		28	91
67	107		27	91
66	106		26	90
65	106		25	90
64	105		24	89
63	105		23	89
62	105		22	88
61	104		21	88
60	104		20	87

Special Report: Retaking the Test: What Are Your Chances at Improving Your Score?

After going through the experience of taking a major test, many test takers feel that once is enough. The test usually comes during a period of transition in the test taker's life, and taking the test is only one of a series of important events. With so many distractions and conflicting recommendations, it may be difficult for a test taker to rationally determine whether or not he should retake the test after viewing his scores.

The importance of the test usually only adds to the burden of the retake decision. However, don't be swayed by emotion. There a few simple questions that you can ask yourself to guide you as you try to determine whether a retake would improve your score:

1. What went wrong? Why wasn't your score what you expected?

Can you point to a single factor or problem that you feel caused the low score? Were you sick on test day? Was there an emotional upheaval in your life that caused a distraction? Were you late for the test or not able to use the full time allotment? If you can point to any of these specific, individual problems, then a retake should definitely be considered.

2. Is there enough time to improve?

Many problems that may show up in your score report may take a lot of time for improvement. A deficiency in a particular math skill may require weeks or months of tutoring and studying to improve. If you have enough time to improve an identified weakness, then a retake should definitely be considered.

3. How will additional scores be used? Will a score average, highest score, or most recent score be used?

Different test scores may be handled completely differently. If you've taken the test multiple times, sometimes your highest score is used, sometimes your average score is computed and used, and sometimes your most recent score is used. Make sure you understand what method will be used to evaluate your scores, and use that to help you determine whether a retake should be considered.

4. Are my practice test scores significantly higher than my actual test score?

If you have taken a lot of practice tests and are consistently scoring at a much higher level than your actual test score, then you should consider a retake. However, if you've taken five practice tests and only one of your scores was higher than your actual test score, or if your practice test scores were only slightly higher than your actual test score, then it is unlikely that you will significantly increase your score.

5. Do I need perfect scores or will I be able to live with this score? Will this score still allow me to follow my dreams?

What kind of score is acceptable to you? Is your current score "good enough?" Do you have to have a certain score in order to pursue the future of your dreams? If you won't be happy with your current score, and there's no way that you could live with it, then you should consider a retake. However, don't get your hopes up. If you are looking for significant improvement, that may or may not be possible. But if you won't be happy otherwise, it is at least worth the effort.

Remember that there are other considerations. To achieve your dream, it is likely that your grades may also be taken into account. A great test score is

Copyright © Mometrix Media. You have been licensed one copy of this document for personal use only. Any other reproduction or redistribution is strictly prohibited. All rights reserved.

usually not the only thing necessary to succeed. Make sure that you aren't overemphasizing the importance of a high test score.

Furthermore, a retake does not always result in a higher score. Some test takers will score lower on a retake, rather than higher. One study shows that one-fourth of test takers will achieve a significant improvement in test score, while one-sixth of test takers will actually show a decrease. While this shows that most test takers will improve, the majority will only improve their scores a little and a retake may not be worth the test taker's effort.

Finally, if a test is taken only once and is considered in the added context of good grades on the part of a test taker, the person reviewing the grades and scores may be tempted to assume that the test taker just had a bad day while taking the test, and may discount the low test score in favor of the high grades. But if the test is retaken and the scores are approximately the same, then the validity of the low scores are only confirmed. Therefore, a retake could actually hurt a test taker by definitely bracketing a test taker's score ability to a limited range.

Special Report: What is Test Anxiety and How to Overcome It?

The very nature of tests caters to some level of anxiety, nervousness or tension, just as we feel for any important event that occurs in our lives. A little bit of anxiety or nervousness can be a good thing. It helps us with motivation, and makes achievement just that much sweeter. However, too much anxiety can be a problem; especially if it hinders our ability to function and perform.

"Test anxiety," is the term that refers to the emotional reactions that some test-takers experience when faced with a test or exam. Having a fear of testing and exams is based upon a rational fear, since the test-taker's performance can shape the course of an academic career. Nevertheless, experiencing excessive fear of examinations will only interfere with the test-takers ability to perform, and his/her chances to be successful.

There are a large variety of causes that can contribute to the development and sensation of test anxiety. These include, but are not limited to lack of performance and worrying about issues surrounding the test.

Lack of Preparation

Lack of preparation can be identified by the following behaviors or situations:

Not scheduling enough time to study, and therefore cramming the night before the test or exam
Managing time poorly, to create the sensation that there is not enough time to do everything

Failing to organize the text information in advance, so that the study material consists of the entire text and not simply the pertinent information

Poor overall studying habits

Worrying, on the other hand, can be related to both the test taker, or many other factors around him/her that will be affected by the results of the test. These include worrying about:

Previous performances on similar exams, or exams in general

How friends and other students are achieving

The negative consequences that will result from a poor grade or failure

There are three primary elements to test anxiety. Physical components, which involve the same typical bodily reactions as those to acute anxiety (to be discussed below). Emotional factors have to do with fear or panic. Mental or cognitive issues concerning attention spans and memory abilities.

Physical Signals

There are many different symptoms of test anxiety, and these are not limited to mental and emotional strain. Frequently there are a range of physical signals that will let a test taker know that he/she is suffering from test anxiety. These bodily changes can include the following:

Perspiring

Sweaty palms

Wet, trembling hands

Nausea

Dry mouth

A knot in the stomach

Headache

Faintness

Muscle tension

Aching shoulders, back and neck

Rapid heart beat

Feeling too hot/cold

To recognize the sensation of test anxiety, a test-taker should monitor him/herself for the following sensations:

The physical distress symptoms as listed above

Emotional sensitivity, expressing emotional feelings such as the need to cry or laugh too much, or a sensation of anger or helplessness

A decreased ability to think, causing the test-taker to blank out or have racing thoughts that are hard to organize or control.

Though most students will feel some level of anxiety when faced with a test or exam, the majority can cope with that anxiety and maintain it at a manageable level. However, those who cannot are faced with a very real and very serious condition, which can and should be controlled for the immeasurable benefit of this sufferer.

Naturally, these sensations lead to negative results for the testing experience. The most common effects of test anxiety have to do with nervousness and mental blocking.

Nervousness

Nervousness can appear in several different levels:

The test-taker's difficulty, or even inability to read and understand the questions on the test

The difficulty or inability to organize thoughts to a coherent form

The difficulty or inability to recall key words and concepts relating to the testing questions (especially essays)

The receipt of poor grades on a test, though the test material was well known by the test taker

Conversely, a person may also experience mental blocking, which involves:

Blanking out on test questions

Only remembering the correct answers to the questions when the test has already finished.

Fortunately for test anxiety sufferers, beating these feelings, to a large degree, has to do with proper preparation. When a test taker has a feeling of preparedness, then anxiety will be dramatically lessened.

The first step to resolving anxiety issues is to distinguish which of the two types of anxiety are being suffered. If the anxiety is a direct result of a lack of preparation, this should be considered a normal reaction, and the anxiety level (as opposed to the test results) shouldn't be anything to worry about. However, if, when adequately prepared, the test-taker still panics, blanks out, or seems to overreact, this is not a fully rational reaction. While this can be considered normal too, there are many ways to combat and overcome these effects.

Remember that anxiety cannot be entirely eliminated, however, there are ways to minimize it, to make the anxiety easier to manage. Preparation is one of the best ways to minimize test anxiety. Therefore the following techniques are wise in order to best fight off any anxiety that may want to build.

To begin with, try to avoid cramming before a test, whenever it is possible. By trying to memorize an entire term's worth of information in one day, you'll be shocking your system, and not giving yourself a very good chance to absorb the information. This is an easy path to anxiety, so for those who suffer from test anxiety, cramming should not even be considered an option.

Instead of cramming, work throughout the semester to combine all of the material which is presented throughout the semester, and work on it gradually as the course goes by, making sure to master the main concepts first, leaving minor details for a week or so before the test.

To study for the upcoming exam, be sure to pose questions that may be on the examination, to gauge the ability to answer them by integrating the ideas from your texts, notes and lectures, as well as any supplementary readings.

If it is truly impossible to cover all of the information that was covered in that particular term, concentrate on the most important portions, that can be covered very well. Learn these concepts as best as possible, so that when the test comes, a goal can be made to use these concepts as presentations of your knowledge.

In addition to study habits, changes in attitude are critical to beating a struggle with test anxiety. In fact, an improvement of the perspective over the entire test-taking experience can actually help a test taker to enjoy studying and therefore improve the overall experience. Be certain not to overemphasize the significance of the grade - know that the result of the test is neither a reflection of self worth, nor is it a measure of intelligence; one grade will not predict a person's future success.

To improve an overall testing outlook, the following steps should be tried:

Keeping in mind that the most reasonable expectation for taking a test is to expect to try to demonstrate as much of what you know as you possibly can. Reminding ourselves that a test is only one test; this is not the only one, and there will be others.

The thought of thinking of oneself in an irrational, all-or-nothing term should be avoided at all costs.

A reward should be designated for after the test, so there's something to look forward to. Whether it be going to a movie, going out to eat, or simply visiting friends, schedule it in advance, and do it no matter what result is expected on the exam.

Test-takers should also keep in mind that the basics are some of the most important things, even beyond anti-anxiety techniques and studying. Never neglect the basic social, emotional and biological needs, in order to try to absorb information. In order to best achieve, these three factors must be held as just as important as the studying itself.

Study Steps

Remember the following important steps for studying:

Maintain healthy nutrition and exercise habits. Continue both your recreational activities and social pass times. These both contribute to your physical and emotional well being.

Be certain to get a good amount of sleep, especially the night before the test, because when you're overtired you are not able to perform to the best of your best ability.

Keep the studying pace to a moderate level by taking breaks when they are needed, and varying the work whenever possible, to keep the mind fresh instead of getting bored.

When enough studying has been done that all the material that can be learned has been learned, and the test taker is prepared for the test, stop studying and do something relaxing such as listening to music, watching a movie, or taking a warm bubble bath.

There are also many other techniques to minimize the uneasiness or apprehension that is experienced along with test anxiety before, during, or even after the examination. In fact, there are a great deal of things that can be done to stop anxiety from interfering with lifestyle and performance. Again, remember that anxiety will not be eliminated entirely, and it shouldn't be. Otherwise that "up" feeling for exams would not exist, and most of us depend on that sensation to perform better than usual. However, this anxiety has to be at a level that is manageable.

Of course, as we have just discussed, being prepared for the exam is half the battle right away. Attending all classes, finding out what knowledge will be expected on the exam, and knowing the exam schedules are easy steps to lowering anxiety. Keeping up with work will remove the need to cram, and efficient study habits will eliminate wasted time. Studying should be done in an ideal location for concentration, so that it is simple to become interested in the material and give it complete attention. A method such as SQ3R (Survey, Question, Read, Recite, Review) is a wonderful key to follow to make sure that the study habits are as effective as possible, especially in the case of learning from a textbook. Flashcards are great techniques for memorization. Learning to

- 79 -

take good notes will mean that notes will be full of useful information, so that less sifting will need to be done to seek out what is pertinent for studying. Reviewing notes after class and then again on occasion will keep the information fresh in the mind. From notes that have been taken summary sheets and outlines can be made for simpler reviewing.

A study group can also be a very motivational and helpful place to study, as there will be a sharing of ideas, all of the minds can work together, to make sure that everyone understands, and the studying will be made more interesting because it will be a social occasion.

Basically, though, as long as the test-taker remains organized and self confident, with efficient study habits, less time will need to be spent studying, and higher grades will be achieved.

To become self confident, there are many useful steps. The first of these is "self talk." It has been shown through extensive research, that self-talk for students who suffer from test anxiety, should be well monitored, in order to make sure that it contributes to self confidence as opposed to sinking the student. Frequently the self talk of test-anxious students is negative or self-defeating, thinking that everyone else is smarter and faster, that they always mess up, and that if they don't do well, they'll fail the entire course. It is important to decreasing anxiety that awareness is made of self talk. Try writing any negative self thoughts and then disputing them with a positive statement instead. Begin self-encouragement as though it was a friend speaking. Repeat positive statements to help reprogram the mind to believing in successes instead of failures.

Helpful Techniques

Other extremely helpful techniques include:

Self-visualization of doing well and reaching goals

While aiming for an "A" level of understanding, don't try to "overprotect" by setting your expectations lower. This will only convince the mind to stop studying in order to meet the lower expectations.

Don't make comparisons with the results or habits of other students. These are individual factors, and different things work for different people, causing different results.

Strive to become an expert in learning what works well, and what can be done in order to improve. Consider collecting this data in a journal.

Create rewards for after studying instead of doing things before studying that will only turn into avoidance behaviors.

Make a practice of relaxing - by using methods such as progressive relaxation, self-hypnosis, guided imagery, etc - in order to make relaxation an automatic sensation.

Work on creating a state of relaxed concentration so that concentrating will take on the focus of the mind, so that none will be wasted on worrying.

Take good care of the physical self by eating well and getting enough sleep.

Plan in time for exercise and stick to this plan.

Beyond these techniques, there are other methods to be used before, during and after the test that will help the test-taker perform well in addition to overcoming anxiety.

Before the exam comes the academic preparation. This involves establishing a study schedule and beginning at least one week before the actual date of the test. By doing this, the anxiety of not having enough time to study for the test will be automatically eliminated. Moreover, this will make the studying a much more effective experience, ensuring that the learning will be an easier process. This relieves much undue pressure on the test-taker.

Summary sheets, note cards, and flash cards with the main concepts and examples of these main concepts should be prepared in advance of the actual studying time. A topic should never be eliminated from this process. By omitting a topic because it isn't expected to be on the test is only setting up the test-taker for anxiety should it actually appear on the exam. Utilize the course syllabus for laying out the topics that should be studied. Carefully go over the notes that were made in class, paying special attention to any of the issues that the professor took special care to emphasize while lecturing in class. In the textbooks, use the chapter review, or if possible, the chapter tests, to begin your review.

It may even be possible to ask the instructor what information will be covered on the exam, or what the format of the exam will be (for example, multiple choice, essay, free form, true-false). Additionally, see if it is possible to find out how many questions will be on the test. If a review sheet or sample test has been offered by the professor, make good use of it, above anything else, for the preparation for the test. Another great resource for getting to know the examination is reviewing tests from previous semesters. Use these tests to review, and aim to achieve a 100% score on each of the possible topics. With a few exceptions, the goal that you set for yourself is the highest one that you will reach.

Take all of the questions that were assigned as homework, and rework them to any other possible course material. The more problems reworked, the more skill and confidence will form as a result. When forming the solution to a problem, write out each of the steps. Don't simply do head work. By doing as many steps on paper as possible, much clarification and therefore confidence will be formed. Do this with as many homework problems as possible, before checking the answers. By checking the answer after each problem, a reinforcement will exist, that will not be on the exam. Study situations should be as exam-like as possible, to prime the test-taker's system for the experience. By waiting to check the answers at the end, a psychological advantage will be formed, to decrease the stress factor.

Another fantastic reason for not cramming is the avoidance of confusion in concepts, especially when it comes to mathematics. 8-10 hours of study will become one hundred percent more effective if it is spread out over a week or at least several days, instead of doing it all in one sitting. Recognize that the human brain requires time in order to assimilate new material, so frequent breaks and a span of study time over several days will be much more beneficial.

Additionally, don't study right up until the point of the exam. Studying should stop a minimum of one hour before the exam begins. This allows the brain to rest and put things in their proper order. This will also provide the time to become as relaxed as possible when going into the examination room. The test-taker will also have time to eat well and eat sensibly. Know that the brain needs food as much as the rest of the body. With enough food and enough sleep, as well as a relaxed attitude, the body and the mind are primed for success.

Avoid any anxious classmates who are talking about the exam. These students only spread anxiety, and are not worth sharing the anxious sentimentalities.

Before the test also involves creating a positive attitude, so mental preparation should also be a point of concentration. There are many keys to creating a positive attitude. Should fears become rushing in, make a visualization of taking the exam, doing well, and seeing an A written on the paper. Write out a list of affirmations that will bring a feeling of confidence, such as "I am doing well in my English class," "I studied well and know my material," "I enjoy this class." Even if the affirmations aren't believed at first, it sends a positive message to the subconscious which will result in an alteration of the overall belief system, which is the system that creates reality.

If a sensation of panic begins, work with the fear and imagine the very worst! Work through the entire scenario of not passing the test, failing the entire course, and dropping out of school, followed by not getting a job, and pushing a shopping cart through the dark alley where you'll live. This will place things into perspective! Then, practice deep breathing and create a visualization of the opposite situation - achieving an "A" on the exam, passing the entire course, receiving the degree at a graduation ceremony.

On the day of the test, there are many things to be done to ensure the best results, as well as the most calm outlook. The following stages are suggested in order to maximize test-taking potential:

Begin the examination day with a moderate breakfast, and avoid any coffee or beverages with caffeine if the test taker is prone to jitters. Even people who are used to managing caffeine can feel jittery or light-headed when it is taken on a test day.

Attempt to do something that is relaxing before the examination begins. As last minute cramming clouds the mastering of overall concepts, it is better to use this time to create a calming outlook.

Be certain to arrive at the test location well in advance, in order to provide time to select a location that is away from doors, windows and other distractions, as well as giving enough time to relax before the test begins.

Keep away from anxiety generating classmates who will upset the sensation of stability and relaxation that is being attempted before the exam.

Should the waiting period before the exam begins cause anxiety, create a self-distraction by reading a light magazine or something else that is relaxing and simple.

During the exam itself, read the entire exam from beginning to end, and find out how much time should be allotted to each individual problem. Once writing the exam, should more time be taken for a problem, it should be abandoned, in order to begin another problem. If there is time at the end, the unfinished problem can always be returned to and completed.

Read the instructions very carefully - twice - so that unpleasant surprises won't follow during or after the exam has ended.

When writing the exam, pretend that the situation is actually simply the completion of homework within a library, or at home. This will assist in forming a relaxed atmosphere, and will allow the brain extra focus for the complex thinking function.

Begin the exam with all of the questions with which the most confidence is felt. This will build the confidence level regarding the entire exam and will begin a quality momentum. This will also create encouragement for trying the problems where uncertainty resides.

Going with the "gut instinct" is always the way to go when solving a problem. Second guessing should be avoided at all costs. Have confidence in the ability to do well.

For essay questions, create an outline in advance that will keep the mind organized and make certain that all of the points are remembered. For multiple choice, read every answer, even if the correct one has been spotted - a better one may exist.

Continue at a pace that is reasonable and not rushed, in order to be able to work carefully. Provide enough time to go over the answers at the end, to check for small errors that can be corrected.

Should a feeling of panic begin, breathe deeply, and think of the feeling of the body releasing sand through its pores. Visualize a calm, peaceful place, and include all of the sights, sounds and sensations of this image. Continue the deep breathing, and take a few minutes to continue this with closed eyes. When all is well again, return to the test.

If a "blanking" occurs for a certain question, skip it and move on to the next question. There will be time to return to the other question later. Get everything done that can be done, first, to guarantee all the grades that can be compiled, and to build all of the confidence possible. Then return to the weaker questions to build the marks from there.

Remember, one's own reality can be created, so as long as the belief is there, success will follow. And remember: anxiety can happen later, right now, there's an exam to be written!

After the examination is complete, whether there is a feeling for a good grade or a bad grade, don't dwell on the exam, and be certain to follow through on the reward that was promised...and enjoy it! Don't dwell on any mistakes that have been made, as there is nothing that can be done at this point anyway.

Additionally, don't begin to study for the next test right away. Do something relaxing for a while, and let the mind relax and prepare itself to begin absorbing information again.

From the results of the exam - both the grade and the entire experience, be certain to learn from what has gone on. Perfect studying habits and work some more on confidence in order to make the next examination experience even better than the last one.

Learn to avoid places where openings occurred for laziness, procrastination and day dreaming.

Use the time between this exam and the next one to better learn to relax, even learning to relax on cue, so that any anxiety can be controlled during the next exam. Learn how to relax the body. Slouch in your chair if that helps. Tighten and then relax all of the different muscle groups, one group at a time, beginning with the feet and then working all the way up to the neck and face. This will ultimately relax the muscles more than they were to begin with. Learn how to breathe deeply and comfortably, and focus on this breathing going in and out as a relaxing thought. With every exhale, repeat the word "relax."

As common as test anxiety is, it is very possible to overcome it. Make yourself one of the test-takers who overcome this frustrating hindrance.

Special Report: How to Overcome Your Fear of Math

If this article started by saying "Math," many of us would feel a shiver crawl up our spines, just by reading that simple word. Images of torturous years in those crippling desks of the math classes can become so vivid to our consciousness that we can almost smell those musty textbooks, and see the smudges of the #2 pencils on our fingers.

If you are still a student, feeling the impact of these sometimes overwhelming classroom sensations, you are not alone if you get anxious at just the thought of taking that compulsory math course. Does your heart beat just that much faster when you have to split the bill for lunch among your friends with a group of your friends? Do you truly believe that you simply don't have the brain for math? Certainly you're good at other things, but math just simply isn't one of them? Have you ever avoided activities, or other school courses because they appear to involve mathematics, with which you're simply not comfortable?

If any one or more of these "symptoms" can be applied to you, you could very well be suffering from a very real condition called "Math Anxiety."

It's not at all uncommon for people to think that they have some sort of math disability or allergy, when in actuality, their block is a direct result of the way in which they were taught math!

In the late 1950's with the dawning of the space age, New Math - a new "fuzzy math" reform that focuses on higher-order thinking, conceptual understanding and solving problems - took the country by storm. It's now becoming ever more clear that teachers were not supplied with the correct, practical and effective way in which they should be teaching new math so that students will understand the methods comfortably. So is it any wonder that so many students struggled so deeply, when their teachers were required to change their entire math systems without the foundation of proper training? Even if you have not been personally, directly affected by that precise event, its impact is still as rampant as ever.

Basically, the math teachers of today are either the teachers who began teaching the new math in the first place (without proper training) or they are the students of the math teachers who taught new math without proper training. Therefore, unless they had a unique, exceptional teacher, their primary, consistent examples of teaching math have been teachers using methods that are not conducive to the general understanding of the entire class. This explains why your discomfort (or fear) of math is not at all rare.

It is very clear why being called up to the chalk board to solve a math problem is such a common example of a terrifying situation for students - and it has very little to do with a fear of being in front of the class. Most of us have had a minimum of one humiliating experience while standing with chalk dusted fingers, with the eyes of every math student piercing through us. These are the images that haunt us all the way through adulthood. But it does not mean that we cannot learn math. It just means that we could be developing a solid case of math anxiety.

But what exactly is math anxiety? It's an very strong emotional sensation of anxiety, panic, or fear that people feel when they think about or must apply their ability to understand mathematics. Sufferers of math anxiety frequently believe that they are incapable of doing activities or taking classes that involve math skills. In fact, some people with math anxiety have developed such a fear that it has become a phobia; aptly named math phobia.

The incidence of math anxiety, especially among college students, but also among high school students, has risen considerably over the last 10 years, and currently this increase shows no signs of slowing down. Frequently students will even chose their college majors and programs based specifically on how little math will be compulsory for the completion of the degree.

The prevalence of math anxiety has become so dramatic on college campuses that many of these schools have special counseling programs that are designed to assist math anxious students to deal with their discomfort and their math problems.

Math anxiety itself is not an intellectual problem, as many people have been lead to believe; it is, in fact, an emotional problem that stems from improper math teaching techniques that have slowly built and reinforced these feelings. However, math anxiety can result in an intellectual problem when its symptoms interfere with a person's ability to learn and understand math.

The fear of math can cause a sort of "glitch" in the brain that can cause an otherwise clever person to stumble over even the simplest of math problems. A study by Dr. Mark H. Ashcraft of Cleveland State University in Ohio showed that college students who usually perform well, but who suffer from math anxiety, will suffer from fleeting lapses in their working memory when they are asked to perform even the most basic mental arithmetic. These same issues regarding memory were not present in the same students when they were required to answer questions that did not involve numbers. This very clearly demonstrated that the memory phenomenon is quite specific to only math.

So what exactly is it that causes this inhibiting math anxiety? Unfortunately it is not as simple as one answer, since math anxiety doesn't have one specific cause.

Frequently math anxiety can result of a student's either negative experience or embarrassment with math or a math teacher in previous years.

These circumstances can prompt the student to believe that he or she is somehow deficient in his or her math abilities. This belief will consistently lead to a poor performance in math tests and courses in general, leading only to confirm the beliefs of the student's inability. This particular phenomenon is referred to as the "self-fulfilling prophecy" by the psychological community. Math anxiety will result in poor performance, rather than it being the other way around.

Dr. Ashcraft stated that math anxiety is a "It's a learned, almost phobic, reaction to math," and that it is not only people prone to anxiety, fear, or panic who can develop math anxiety. The image alone of doing math problems can send the blood pressure and heart rate to race, even in the calmest person.

The study by Dr. Ashcraft and his colleague Elizabeth P. Kirk, discovered that students who suffered from math anxiety were frequently stumped by issues of even the most basic math rules, such as "carrying over" a number, when performing a sum, or "borrowing" from a number when doing a subtraction. Lapses such as this occurred only on working memory questions involving numbers.

To explain the problem with memory, Ashcraft states that when math anxiety begins to take its effect, the sufferer experiences a rush of thoughts, leaving little room for the focus required to perform even the simplest of math problems. He stated that "you're draining away the energy you need for solving the problem by worrying about it."

The outcome is a "vicious cycle," for students who are sufferers of math anxiety. As math anxiety is developed, the fear it promotes stands in the way of learning, leading to a decrease in self-confidence in the ability to perform even simple arithmetic.

A large portion of the problem lies in the ways in which math is taught to students today. In the US, students are frequently taught the rules of math, but rarely will they learn why a specific approach to a math problems work. Should students be provided with a foundation of "deeper understanding" of math, it may prevent the development of phobias.

Another study that was published in the Journal of Experimental Psychology by Dr. Jamie Campbell and Dr. Qilin Xue of the University of Saskatchewan in Saskatoon, Canada, reflected the same concepts. The researchers in this study looked at university students who were educated in Canada and China, discovering that the Chinese students could generally outperform the Canadian-educated students when it came to solving complex math problems involving procedural knowledge - the ability to know how to solve a math problem, instead of simply having ideas memorized.

A portion of this result seemed to be due to the use of calculators within both elementary and secondary schools; while Canadians frequently used them, the Chinese students did not.

However, calculators were not the only issue. Since Chinese-educated students also outperformed Canadian-educated students in complex math, it is suggested that cultural factors may also have an impact. However, the short-cut of using the calculator may hinder the development of the problem solving skills that are key to performing well in math.

Though it is critical that students develop such fine math skills, it is easier said than done. It would involve an overhaul of the training among all elementary and secondary educators, changing the education major in every college.

Math Myths

One problem that contributes to the progression of math anxiety, is the belief of many math myths. These erroneous math beliefs include the following:

Men are better in math than women - however, research has failed to demonstrate that there is any difference in math ability between the sexes. There is a single best way to solve a math problem - however, the majority of math problems can be solved in a number of different ways. By saying that there is only one way to solve a math problem, the thinking and creative skills of the student are held back.

Some people have a math mind, and others do not - in truth, the majority of people have much more potential for their math capabilities than they believe of themselves.

It is a bad thing to count by using your fingers - counting by using fingers has actually shown that an understanding of arithmetic has been established. People who are skilled in math can do problems quickly in their heads - in actuality, even math professors will review their example problems before they teach them in their classes.

The anxieties formed by these myths can frequently be perpetuated by a range of mind games that students seem to play with themselves. These math mind games include the following beliefs:

I don't perform math fast enough - actually everyone has a different rate at which he or she can learn. The speed of the solving of math problems is not important as long as the student can solve it.

I don't have the mind for math - this belief can inhibit a student's belief in him or herself, and will therefore interfere with the student's real ability to learn math.

I got the correct answer, but it was done the wrong way - there is no single best way to complete a math problem. By believing this, a student's creativity and overall understanding of math is hindered.

If I can get the correct answer, then it is too simple - students who suffer from math anxiety frequently belittle their own abilities when it comes to their math capabilities.

Math is unrelated to my "real" life - by freeing themselves of the fear of math, math anxiety sufferers are only limiting their choices and freedoms for the rest of their life.

Fortunately, there are many ways to help those who suffer from math anxiety. Since math anxiety is a learned, psychological response to doing or thinking about math, that interferes with the sufferer's ability to understand and perform math, it is not at all a reflection of the sufferer's true math sills and abilities.

Helpful Strategies

Many strategies and therapies have been developed to help students to overcome their math anxious responses. Some of these helpful strategies include the following:

Reviewing and learning basic arithmetic principles, techniques and methods. Frequently math anxiety is a result of the experience of many students with early negative situations, and these students have never truly developed a strong base in basic arithmetic, especially in the case of multiplication and fractions. Since math is a discipline that is built on an accumulative foundation, where the concepts are built upon gradually from simpler concepts, a student who has not achieved a solid basis in arithmetic will experience difficulty in learning higher order math. Taking a remedial math course, or a short math course that focuses on arithmetic can often make a considerable difference in reducing the anxious response that math anxiety sufferers have with math.

Becoming aware of any thoughts, actions and feelings that are related to math and responses to math. Math anxiety has a different effect on different students. Therefore it is very important to become familiar with any reactions that the math anxiety sufferer may have about him/herself and the situation when math has been encountered. If the sufferer becomes aware of any irrational or unrealistic thoughts, it's possible to better concentrate on replacing these thoughts with more positive and realistic ones.

Find help! Math anxiety, as we've mentioned, is a learned response, that is reinforced repeatedly over a period of time, and is therefore not something that can be eliminated instantaneously. Students can more effectively reduce their anxious responses with the help of many different services that are readily available. Seeking the assistance of a psychologist or counselor, especially one with a specialty in math anxiety, can assist the sufferer in performing an analysis of his/her psychological response to math, as well as learning anxiety management skills, and developing effective coping strategies. Other great tools are tutors, classes that teach better abilities to take better notes in math class, and other math learning aids.

Learning the mathematic vocabulary will instantly provide a better chance for understanding new concepts. One major issue among students is the lack of understanding of the terms and vocabulary that are common jargon within math classes. Typically math classes will utilize words in a completely different way from the way in which they are utilized in all other subjects. Students easily mistake their lack of understanding the math terms with their mathematical abilities.

Learning anxiety reducing techniques and methods for anxiety management. Anxiety greatly interferes with a student's ability to concentrate, think clearly, pay attention, and remember new concepts. When these same students can learn to relax, using anxiety management techniques, the student can regain his or her ability to control his or her emotional and physical symptoms of anxiety that interfere with the capabilities of mental processing.

Working on creating a positive overall attitude about mathematics. Looking at math with a positive attitude will reduce anxiety through the building of a positive attitude.

Learning to self-talk in a positive way. Pep talking oneself through a positive self talk can greatly assist in overcoming beliefs in math myths or the mind games that may be played. Positive self-talking is an effective way to replace the negative thoughts - the ones that create the anxiety. Even if the sufferer doesn't believe the statements at first, it plants a positive seed in the subconscious, and allows a positive outlook to grow.

Beyond this, students should learn effective math class, note taking and studying techniques. Typically, the math anxious students will avoid asking questions to save themselves from embarrassment. They will sit in the back of classrooms, and refrain from seeking assistance from the professor. Moreover, they will put off studying for math until the very last moment, since it causes them such substantial discomfort. Alone, or a combination of these negative behaviors work only to reduce the anxiety of the students, but in reality, they are actually building a substantially more intense anxiety.

There are many different positive behaviors that can be adopted by math anxious students, so that they can learn to better perform within their math classes.

Sit near the front of the class. This way, there will be fewer distractions, and there will be more of a sensation of being a part of the topic of discussion. If any questions arise, ASK! If one student has a question, then there are certain to be others who have the same question but are too nervous to ask - perhaps because they have not yet learned how to deal with their own math anxiety.

Seek extra help from the professor after class or during office hours.

Prepare, prepare, prepare - read textbook material before the class, do the homework and work out any problems available within the textbook. Math skills are developed through practice and repetition, so the more practice and repetition, the better the math skills.

Review the material once again after class, to repeat it another time, and to reinforce the new concepts that were learned.

Beyond these tactics that can be taken by the students themselves, teachers and parents need to know that they can also have a large impact on the reduction of math anxiety within students.

As parents and teachers, there is a natural desire to help students to learn and understand how they will one day utilize different math techniques within their everyday lives. But when the student or teacher displays the symptoms of a person who has had nightmarish memories regarding math, where hesitations then develop in the instruction of students, these fears are automatically picked up by the students and commonly adopted as their own.

However, it is possible for teachers and parents to move beyond their own fears to better educate students by overcoming their own hesitations and learning to enjoy math.

Begin by adopting the outlook that math is a beautiful, imaginative or living thing. Of course, we normally think of mathematics as numbers that can be added or subtracted, multiplied or divided, but that is simply the beginning of it.

By thinking of math as something fun and imaginative, parents and teachers can teach children different ways to manipulate numbers, for example in balancing a checkbook. Parents rarely tell their children that math is everywhere around us; in nature, art, and even architecture. Usually, this is because they were never shown these relatively simple connections. But that pattern can break very simply through the participation of parents and teachers.

The beauty and hidden wonders of mathematics can easily be emphasized through a focus that can open the eyes of students to the incredible mathematical patterns that arise everywhere within the natural world. Observations and discussions can be made into things as fascinating as spider webs, leaf patterns, sunflowers and even coastlines. This makes math not only beautiful, but also inspiring and (dare we say) fun!

Pappas Method

For parents and teachers to assist their students in discovering the true wonders of mathematics, the techniques of Theoni Pappas can easily be applied, as per her popular and celebrated book "Fractals, Googols and Other Mathematical Tales." Pappas used to be a math phobia sufferer and created a fascinating step-by-step program for parents and teachers to use in order to teach students the joy of math.

Her simple, constructive step-by-step program goes as follows:

Don't let your fear of math come across to your kids - Parents must be careful not to perpetuate the mathematical myth - that math is only for specially talented "math types." Strive not to make comments like; "they don't like math" or "I have never been good at math." When children overhear comments like these from their primary role models they begin to dread math before even considering a chance of experiencing its wonders. It is important to encourage your children to read and explore the rich world of mathematics, and to practice mathematics without imparting negative biases.

Don't immediately associate math with computation (counting) - It is very important to realize that math is not just numbers and computations, but a realm of exciting ideas that touch every part of our lives -from making a telephone call to how the hair grows on someone's head. Take your children outside and point out real objects that display math concepts. For example, show them the symmetry of a leaf or angles on a building. Take a close look at the spirals in a spider web or intricate patterns of a snowflake.

Help your child understand why math is important - Math improves problem solving, increases competency and should be applied in different ways. It's the same as reading. You can learn the basics of reading without ever enjoying a novel. But, where's the excitement in that? With math, you could stop with the basics. But why when there is so much more to be gained by a fuller Understanding? Life is so much more enriching when we go beyond the basics. Stretch your children's minds to become involved in mathematics in ways that will not only be practical but also enhance their lives.

Make math as "hands on" as possible - Mathematicians participate in mathematics. To really experience math encourage your child to dig in and tackle problems in creative ways. Help them learn how to manipulate numbers using concrete references they understand as well as things they can see or touch. Look for patterns everywhere, explore shapes and symmetries. How many octagons do you see each day on the way to the grocery store? Play math puzzles and games and then encourage your child to try to invent their own. And, whenever possible, help your child realize a mathematical conclusion with real and tangible results. For example, measure out a full glass of juice with a measuring cup and then ask your child to drink half. Measure what is left. Does it measure half of a cup?

Read books that make math exciting:
Fractals, Googols and Other Mathematical Tales introduces an animated cat who explains fractals, tangrams and other mathematical concepts you've probably never heard of to children in terms they can understand. This book can double as a great text book by using one story per lesson.

A Wrinkle in Time is a well-loved classic, combining fantasy and science.

The Joy of Mathematics helps adults explore the beauty of mathematics that is all around.

The Math Curse is an amusing book for 4-8 year olds.

The Gnarly Gnews is a free, humorous bi-monthly newsletter on mathematics.

The Phantom Tollbooth is an Alice in Wonderland-style adventure into the worlds of words and numbers.

Use the internet to help your child explore the fascinating world of mathematics.

Web Math provides a powerful set of math-solvers that gives you instant answers to the stickiest problems.

Math League has challenging math materials and contests for fourth grade and above.

Silver Burdett Ginn Mathematics offers Internet-based math activities for grades K-6.

The Gallery of Interactive Geometry is full of fascinating, interactive geometry activities.

Math is very much like a language of its own. And like any second language, it will get rusty if it is not practiced enough. For that reason, students should always be looking into new ways to keep understanding and brushing up on their math skills, to be certain that foundations do not crumble, inhibiting the learning of new levels of math.

There are many different books, services and websites that have been developed to take the fear out of math, and to help even the most uncertain student develop self confidence in his or her math capabilities.

There is no reason for math or math classes to be a frightening experience, nor should it drive a student crazy, making them believe that they simply don't have the "math brain" that is needed to solve certain problems.

There are friendly ways to tackle such problems and it's all a matter of dispelling myths and creating a solid math foundation.

Concentrate on re-learning the basics and feeling better about yourself in math, and you'll find that the math brain you've always wanted, was there all along.

Special Report: Additional Bonus Material

Due to our efforts to try to keep this book to a manageable length, we've created a link that will give you access to all of your additional bonus material.

Please visit http://www.mo-media.com/secretary/bonuses to access the information.